little threads

and other object lessons for children

Harvey Daniel Moore II

Nashville—**Abingdon Press**—New York

Library of Congress Cataloging in Publication Data

Moore. Harvey Daniel, 1942-
    Little threads, and other object lessons for
children.
    1. Children's sermons. I. Title.
BV4315.M624   252   73-21959

ISBN 0-687-22169-2

MANUFACTURED BY THE PARTHENON PRESS AT
NASHVILLE, TENNESSEE, UNITED STATES OF AMERICA

It is my hope that this little book will help make Jesus and his message real to children. For that reason it is dedicated to the two people who made him real to me:

Harvey and Ruth Moore

My Parents

Contents

Preface

In all the worship activities of the church, I have found nothing more quickly accepted or enjoyed by all the people than the children's sermon.

Like any other activity, it can be approached in a number of ways. The most important point to remember while choosing a method for delivery is that the children's sermon is not simply a means of pacifying the requests of some parents. It can be, and in many congregations is, one of the high points of the worship experience.

It illustrates to the adults of the congregation that the church takes seriously its commission to teach the children and make them feel that they are a part of the church family.

The sermon itself also serves as a valid and understandable parable for the adult congregation. Too often the pastor forgets that it is the meangingful illustration that will be remembered by his hearers long after the logical development of his sermon is forgotten.

The most important function of the children's sermon, however, is to speak to the children in a way that shows them they are an important part of what is happening.

Several simple steps may be taken by the pastor to greatly enhance that feeling.

First of all, call the children forward and let them gather around you as you talk with them. I have seen several pastors who call the children to the front pews and then deliver their sermon from the pulpit. No doubt the message is valid, but the deeper message of personal contact is lost. I have found it much more rewarding for myself and the children if I sit on the chancel steps with the children sitting in a group on the floor around me. It gives a much closer and friendlier atmosphere.

Second, talk *with* the children. It is nice to give them a monologue in classic sermon form (and much safer because they can't ask questions), but again, much of the personal contact and involvement is lost. In the following talks the questions and comments of the children play a vital part in getting the message across. Indeed, in many instances the sermon is actually carried by the children. They go away feeling that they have honestly had a conversation *with,* not just another lecture *by,* someone.

Third, the use of the object and its application during the week are important. Several years ago I developed the habit of closing with a referral to

8

the object. A simple comment like: "So this week, everytime you see a comb remember . . ." It has been a very sobering experience over the years to discover the great number of not only children but also adults who do just that!

The children's sermon has become one of the most important parts of the service, I believe, for just the reasons mentioned, and these suggestions should be followed or at least tried by the reader.

1. Sit down with the children and let them be close and informal.
2. Talk *with* them, not just *at* them. Make them a part of what is being done.
3. Give them a specific thought, related to the object, to take home and apply.

When these steps are taken, one of the most rewarding aspects of the ministry will be opened to you.

Lost and Found

Text: *Luke 15:3-7.*

Object: *Something you have made.*

I have a real problem this morning. I lost something that is very important to me. Will you help me find it? I know it is around here somewhere. Let's look for it together.

(Spend about thirty seconds searching with the children.)

Here it is. I found it. Now you can all see what it is. I guess you think it isn't much. As I told you, though, if I lost it, I would miss it because I made it. Maybe some of you can remember things that you have made. You know that after you spend time planning and then actually making those plans a reality, you feel very close to what you have made. You have a special feeling about it.

Have you ever thought that God feels that way about you? We all know that God made us. The Bible tells us that God even knows how many hairs we have on our head. If anything were to happen to us, or if we were ever to begin to wander away from God, then he would miss us and try to bring us back, just as I missed the little clay man that I made and went looking for him.

That was what Jesus was talking about when he told the story of the shepherd who loved each of his sheep. He loved them so much that when he saw one was missing, he didn't ask if it was a big one, or if it was the prettiest one. He didn't even ask if it was a smart sheep or a good sheep. He only said he would find it and bring it home where it would be safe. He would go out and look for it because he loved it.

That is the same way we just looked for the little clay man I made. You remember, we didn't look for him because he was beautiful or even because he was useful. We looked for him because I made him and I like him.

Sometimes we feel that if we do something wrong or if we are not as good as we should be, then God will not love us or want us. That is when we need to remember that Jesus said he is like the shepherd who goes out looking for sheep who have strayed away.

God always looks for us, not because we are so good, but because he made us and he loves us.

Having Faith

Text: *Hebrews 11:1.*

Object: *A can of food and the label. Have the label off the can.*

How many of you have ever helped your mother go shopping or cook dinner? If you have, I am sure you have seen her select or open one of these (Hold up the label-less can.)

We all know that food comes in this kind of can. Now let me ask you one question. What is in this can?

(Let the children make a few suggestions.)

It is a problem, isn't it? We cannot see through the metal. If we shake it, we don't learn anything. We could open it, but then if it is not what we want we have another problem. How do we know what is in it? We do not know, do we? I guess it will have to remain a mystery. (Pause for a few seconds.)

What if I told you that the first time I saw this can it had this paper wrapped around it? (Hold up the label.) Oh. That solves everything. Now we all know that there are peas in this can. Are you sure? I mean, how do you really know? The label says so, but you still cannot see inside the can. Are you willing to believe it just because the label says so? Why?

(Pause and let a few of the children give their answers.)

That's right. You know that every time you have opened a can in the past, you found that the label was correct. What it told you on the outside was true about the inside. You could say that the labels have never failed you and so you have come to trust them. Now when you see a picture on the outside of a can you "know" what is on the inside, even if you cannot really see it.

When we talk about Jesus we call that kind of trust "faith." We do not always know how things will turn out in our lives, just as we cannot actually see what is inside this can. But we do know that Jesus has never failed those who are near him, and that everything he said is true and we can depend on it. In a word, we can trust him!

Faith, then, is knowing that God will work things out for the best, even when we do not understand how he does it.

From now on, every time you see a can and a label, remember how you trust that label and how much more you can trust God.

Pile It On

Text: *Ephesians 4:11-12.*

Object: *Several large toys.*

This morning I am going to need several volunteers.

(Choose one of the children.)

Would you stand next to me and hold this, please? Now (choose another child) would you hold this one, and stand next to him?

(Continue to pick children, giving each of them a bulky toy to hold. The line should involve at least ten children, or as many as possible if fewer than that.)

Each of you has a toy in your hands. Would it be any problem, now, if I asked you to take all of them to the back of the sanctuary? Of course not. Each of you could carry what you have. No one would be overloaded.

Before you leave to carry them to the back, there is something we need to do. John, you look a little tired this morning. Why don't you give your toy to Patti to carry for you? Bill, we are about ready to carry them off, but I know you have a lot to do. You give yours to Patti too. Jane, I know you are not feeling well. You rest and let Patti carry yours.

15

Nancy, I know you would like to help, but I know you have guests and would like to sit with them. You give yours to Patti and have a seat also.

(Each child should give the toy he is holding to Patti when you ask him to; then he should be seated. By this time Patti should be totally over-loaded. If not, continue to pile it on her, using the various excuses that are common for not being able to help in church work. Patti will soon have so many toys that she will begin to drop some of them. The point will be obvious. After she has wrestled a losing battle with her load, have all the children sit back down by you.)

I think you all see what I am trying to say this morning. As long as everyone was carrying his or her fair share, no one had a problem. As soon as we started making excuses and passing all the work to Patti, the job of carrying everything became a problem.

The same thing is true with the church. If we all carry our share we can do the Lord's work and the church can be all the things Jesus wants it to be. If we begin making excuses and passing our share on to others, pretty soon a few folks are doing everything and a lot of the Lord's work gets dropped and left undone. Even if our excuse is a good one, the result is still the same. All the work still gets put off on a few people. How much better it is when all of us do our part. Then it all gets done.

This week, let's each find our special job and try our best to do it right. Whenever you are tempted to say you cannot do your part, stop for a second and remember how Patti looked trying to carry all those toys by herself. Jesus needs all of us to be his helpers if his work is going to get done.

It's What's Inside That Counts!

Text: *Genesis 2:7.*

Object: *Flowerpots and a package of flower seeds.*

This morning I would like you to help me plant some flowers. As you can see from the picture on the package, when they grow they will be pretty blue flowers. What we are supposed to do is place a few seeds in the soil of each pot and let them grow. God's sunlight and water will do the rest.

I also have several flowerpots here. I think we can use this first one. It is all clean and pretty.

(Spend some time looking over the rest of the pots very carefully.)

I think we can use the next two as well. We will not be able to use this fourth one, though. As you can see, it has some orange paint on the outside of it.

What? Did someone say that makes no difference? Are you going to tell me that I can grow God's blue flowers in a pot with orange marks on the outside? How can that be? Of course! The beauty of the flower depends on the seed, not on the color of the pot.

If that is true, can I even use this pot with a little

chip on the side of it? I can? You mean that God's seeds will grow even if the pot is not perfect? Of course they will.

Now, all that seems a little silly, doesn't it? Yet, do you know that sometimes you and I tend to make that same kind of mistake about people? We know that God puts his Spirit in all people, and that is what is important.

Instead of looking for God's Spirit, however, we too often tend to look at the outward appearance of a person. If he does not look exactly as we want him to, if he is a different color or does things in a different way, we think he ought to be set aside. Yet we know that that is not true, is it?

The important thing is what is on the inside of a person. And what is inside is God's Spirit. Sometimes it is hard to see—like a seed under the dirt in the flowerpot—but it is still there, and it is still growing. Our job is to help it grow, not to criticize the things that are not important.

For the next few days, let's all try something special. Every time you see a person, stop and remind yourself that God's Spirit is in him, trying to grow. Then ask God what you can do to help him. It is like watering the seed in the flowerpot. Remember, it is the Spirit inside that is important, not just what can be seen.

Going Along
with the Crowd

Text: *I Timothy 1:3-7.*

Object: *A paper sack.*

I have something here that no one in the whole world has ever seen before. No one has ever seen it because it is invisible. Do you know what "invisible" means? It means something is not visible, it cannot be seen. (Pause for a second or two to let them think about that part.)

I'll bet if you try, though, some of you can see it.

(Hold up your thumb and index finger as if you were holding a small ball. Give several of them time to "look" at it.)

Can you see it? I'll bet some of you did. You can see it already! (A few of them will begin to nod their heads.)

Now watch this!

(Hold the paper sack in one hand, with your hand on the bottom. Pretend to toss the "ball" into the air and catch it in the sack. The effect of catching the ball is given by thumping your finger on the bottom of the sack. Take the ball out and show it to the children again. A few more will see it this time. Repeat the toss and catch, with sound effects, two or three more times until most of the children see the ball.)

Some of you thought I was just teasing, but now you have seen me throw the ball into the air, and you have heard it come down. Now I'll bet several of you can see it. There it is. Take a good look.

(Hold your fingers out again, as if holding a ball. Give the children time to compare notes on the size and color of the ball if they want.)

I have just one more question to ask. Did you really see a ball just now? No. You all know that there is no invisible ball here, don't you? Yet while I was talking and hitting my finger against the sack, all of you were saying that you saw a ball, even though you didn't. Do you know why you were saying that? Sometimes it seems easier to go along and agree with what everyone else says than to say something different. Often we do that even when we know the other person is wrong.

It is not wrong to be like other people, but we should not let ourselves agree with something that is not true just because we want to be like everyone else.

While we are in school or playing, there are always people who are trying to tell us things. Some of them will tell us things that are not right, and we know they are not right. When that happens we should not stand by and agree, the way we did just

21

now, pretending to see a ball that we knew was not there. We should speak up for what we know is true.

This week, when we hear something new, or when someone says, "You should believe such-and-such," let's spend some time thinking about it. If it is not true, or if we do not believe it, let's not pretend to. From now on let's make a habit of standing up for what we believe.

Who Stands
Behind You?

Text: *Titus 3:5-7.*

Object: *A dollar bill and a piece of green paper about the same size.*

I know that all of you recognize this. It is a piece of green paper. Can you tell me some of the things we can do with a piece of paper like this? Right. We can draw on it. We can make an airplane out of it. We can do several things with it. Now, what happens if I do this?

(Crumple the paper into a small ball in your hand.)

Now what can we do with it? That is right: nothing! We may as well throw it away.

Now I want to show you another piece of green paper.

(Hold out a crisp dollar bill.)

What is this one good for? That's right. We can buy things with it. We can save it. We can help other people with it. We can do all sorts of things with it.

Now, what if I crumple it all into a ball like the other piece of green paper? Now I guess we ought to throw it away also. No? You mean it is still good for something? I had to throw the last piece of paper away when it was crumpled like this. Why is this one still good if the other one was not? Because it is money? What makes it money? Oh, the picture on it. What if I draw a picture like that on the first piece of paper? Will that help? Of course not.

The reason the money is still of value is because of what stands behind it. The United States Government says that it will guarantee the worth of this piece of paper. Even if it is wrinkled and worn, it is still of value when we turn it in. Not because the paper itself is still in perfect condition, but because we can claim the promise the Government makes to stand behind it.

Did you know that the same is true about us and God? When we become Christians, we form a very special relationship or friendship with God. As we get older and go through life, sometimes we start looking like this piece of paper. We get smudged up or torn a little along the way. We may even get pretty far from where we should be. But there is one important thing to remember always. God has given us his promise. He is ready to redeem us and make us what we should be anytime we let him. The Bible says Jesus has given us his grace, and as

Christians we are his. We will never be thrown away, because God stands behind us.

That is an important thing to remember. God's promise stands with us always, and he will redeem us in the end—not because we are still perfect, but because he loves us.

Safe in God's Hand

Text: *John 10:28.*

Object: *A toy man, small enough to fit in a closed fist.*

As you can see, I have here a very small statue of a man. He is so small that he fits right in the palm of my hand. Now as I set him there, I want to show you something.

(Make a first around the man.)

You can see that I have a good, tight hold on him. I want some of you to try to open my hand and get the man out.

(Hold out your hand and let several of the children try to open it. Of course, they are small children and will not be able to do it. After they make several vigorous but unsuccessful attempts to open your hand, continue with the story.)

You can see that it is impossible for you to get my hand open, because I want to hold on to what is inside. I think you would all agree that the little man is pretty safe!

Did you know that Jesus said the same thing about us? He said that God has placed each one of us in his hand. Of course, God's hand does not look just like my hand, but what Jesus was saying was that God has placed himself about us, and that there is no power anywhere strong enough to take us away from him. God loves us, and he holds us close to him.

I want you to remember that the next time you feel afraid or you feel that something is trying to draw you away from God. You are in God's hand, and nothing can pry you loose from his love.

The Wheat
and the Chaff

Text: *Matthew 13:24-30.*

Object: *Stalks of wheat, grass, and various weeds.*

As you all know, many people came to Jesus to ask him questions about things that troubled them. They had a question then that bothers many people today, maybe even some of us here. They asked Jesus, "Why do people who do bad things seem to get along all right and nothing seems to happen to them?" Have you ever wondered about that?

Jesus had an answer, and I am going to show what he did. You see that I have two stalks of wheat. We all know that the farmer plants the wheat and cares for it. When it ripens, like these two stalks, the farmer cuts it and takes the kernels for grinding into flour for bread and things.

There is a problem, however. While the wheat is growing, sometimes other things begin to grow with it. This stalk of grass, for example, looks a lot like wheat, but it is not good for eating. This other grass also grows with the wheat, and it is not good for eating either. Yet all three of them grow and live together in the same field, just as good and bad people live in the same world all mixed together.

Jesus said all these grow together until the time for the harvest comes. Then something happens. Now watch. The good thing we want out of all this is is the wheat kernel. I take all the stalks of wheat and grass and crush them together between my hands like this. Now I rub it around for awhile —and look.

(Hold out your hand, which will be full of stubble.)

It still looks all mixed up. Watch and see what happens.

(Blow the chaff away.)

One puff of wind and the chaff is gone, and the wheat kernel is all that is left.

Jesus said that is the way it will happen with people. We will all live together, but when the judgment does come, we will be separated like the wheat and chaff. The fact that people who are doing wrong now continue to live and act as if nothing will happen, is not really important. We need to think about how we will fare when our actions and thoughts are judged by Christ. Will we be blown away like the chaff, or will we be a part of God's wheat? It is an important thought for us to ponder. It is also important when we decide how we will act. We grow for him, and he helps to turn us into the very best persons we can be.

29

Little Threads

Text: *Jeremiah 13:23.*

Object: *Some pieces of thread, a piece of string, and some rope.*

As you can see, I have some threads here in my hand. You all know that threads are not very strong. Would one of you boys come here, please, and hold your wrists together? Now watch. I will wrap this thread one time around his wrists. Now see if you can break that off. Good! That was no problem. Let's do it again, and this time I will wrap the thread around his wrists several times. It is still fairly easy to get loose, but not like the first time.

As you know, if we weave several strands of thread together we get a string. Now let me put some of this string around your wrists.

(Let the boy struggle with this one for awhile, but be sure it is loose enough for him to get free in a few seconds.)

If we weave a few strands of string together, what do we get? That's right: a rope! Let's see what happens when I put this rope around your wrists.

(Tie him firmly so he cannot get loose.)

This time the bonds are just too strong. You cannot get loose no matter how hard you try. Yet we know that all rope is, is just a lot of little weak threads woven together.

Do you think there is something we can learn from this thread and rope? Of course!

The thread is just like a habit. When we do something once, it is like the first thread. It is easy to break or to stop doing it. The more we do it, however, the harder it is to stop. We do not intend to do it all the time, but the more we repeat the act or thought, the stronger it becomes. It is like the threads being woven into a rope. It gets stronger and stronger with each new thread. Pretty soon it is like a rope around us, and we cannot get free!

The lesson, then, is this. Whenever we find ourselves doing something, we need to ask, Is this a thing Jesus would do? If it is not, then we should stop while it is still like a thread, and never let it get strong enough to control us. That way we control our habits; they do not control us.

Some Habits
Are Good

Text: *John 13:15.*

Object: *Rope.*

I would like a volunteer to come forward this morning. I am going to tie your hands, then I want to explain something.

Last week we talked about how threads are easy to break until they are woven into ropes. Then we said the same thing was true about habits. The first time we do something we can stop easily, like breaking the thread, but if we keep repeating the act over and over again, it becomes a habit and is like the rope: hard to break.

As you can see, our volunteer has a "habit" tied round his wrists. How do you like that? It is a problem, isn't it? You would be better off if you did not have that wrapped around you, wouldn't you? It would seem that the best thing we could do is stay away from these. (Hold up the rope.)

Before we finish though, let's think about one more situation. What if we were at the top of a big cliff, and I asked you to climb down? That would be dangerous, wouldn't it? In fact, you probably would not want to do it. Would it make you feel better if I said I would tie a rope around you, so that if you happened to slip or fall I could catch you? Surely it would. In that case the rope would be a good thing to have!

We can see now that a rope tied one way can be a problem. If it is tied another way, it can be a great help. It is the same way with habits. Some of them are bad habits, or problems. They get us into trouble. Others are good habits. They protect us and keep us going on the right path, even when we are tempted to slip or go astray.

Good habits are formed just like a lifeline rope— by weaving lots of little actions together, over and over again. All we have to do to form the kinds of habits that will become lifelines is to have our parents read us the stories of Jesus. Then we do our very best to act the way he did.

At first we start out slowly, as if weaving threads together to make a rope. Gradually, however, as we do it over and over, it becomes the way we act automatically. It becomes a strong part of us, like the rope. Then later, when we are tempted to slip, we discover that the good habit is strong inside us, and we are held close to what is right.

This week, let's talk with our parents and see what good habits we can follow and begin to weave them together. It is the lifeline that holds us safe and close to God in times of trouble.

God's Guiding Hands

Text: *Jeremiah 18:1-6.*

Object: *A large lump of clay.*

You can all see that I have a ball of clay this morning. I know you have all made things from clay, but did you know that the prophet Jeremiah had some interesting things to say about working with clay?

Watch carefully, and I will show you what God showed Jeremiah.

(While you talk, be forming a small bowl or vase from the clay in your hand.)

God told Jeremiah to go down to the potter's shop and watch. This is what he saw. The potter took the clay and began to mold it into the form of a vase. Sometimes, however, when a vase is being formed a problem comes up. You can see here, in the one I am making, a small hole in the side of it.

(Let the children watch you work on the vase to try to get the hole filled and the form corrected. After several seconds of trying unsuccessfully you appear to give up.)

That is simply not going to work. It looks as though that vase is ruined. Now I will have to start over. I guess I will have to throw this clay away, right? No? What should I do? Of course! I do not throw perfectly good clay away, I just make it back into a ball and start over again. This time I work the clay, and it comes out the way I want it to. That is what God showed Jeremiah. He told Jeremiah that God does the same thing with us. When we become Christians we give our lives to God. He becomes the potter, the one who molds us. Sometimes, however, a flaw appears. We may do something wrong, or we fail to obey God in some way, and we know that, like the vase (hold up the clay), we are not what we should be. That is when God calls to us to begin all over again. He does not just throw us away. He works with us over and over again, always trying to make us the very best we can be.

This week, when you hear that small voice inside you say do this or don't do that, remember that God is trying to help you by his guidance, and follow the guidance he gives.

Little Things
Can Be Big

Text: *I Timothy 6:10.*

Object: *A dime.*

This is a dime! Can everyone see it? Everyone knows what a dime is, right? It looks small, doesn't it? Did you know that a dime can change size? I know some of you do not believe me, so let me show you what I mean.

Let's pick out something very large, like the pulpit. Now, if we set the dime next to the pulpit it looks very small, doesn't it? Watch carefully.

(Choose a child to stand next to you. Ask him to close one eye, and explain that you are slowly going to move the dime closer to his open eye, but that you will not touch him. Then continue with the lesson as you move the dime toward the child's eye.)

Tell us what seems to be happening. It looks now as if the dime is getting larger. In fact, the closer it gets to your eye, the larger it looks. Look what happens now.

(Hold the dime very close to the child's eye.)

Now what do you see? That is right, only the dime. It looks as if the dime is the biggest thing in the world. Now as I begin to move it away, it seems to be getting smaller. When I hold it down in my hand again, we can see how small it really is.

Do you know what very important lesson our little experiment teaches? What we are really learning is how money can come to be the biggest thing in our life. If we keep it where it should be, it is something to use for God and others. If we let it get too close to us or become the most important thing in our lives, it begins to blot out every other thing around us. It is not long before all we can see or think about is money.

As followers of Jesus, we have to ask ourselves constantly, What does money mean to us? Is it a tool to use, or is it the only interest we have? If we are not careful, it can become so close to us and seem so important to us that it will shut out everything and everyone else.

The Bible says that the *love* of money is the root of all evil. That does not mean that money is bad, but rather that it can become a real problem when we begin to love it more than we love God and other people.

Amazing Grace

Text: *Ephesians 2:5.*

Object: *A glass and a magic jug. This is a small plastic jug with hollow sides. It is filled with water. When it is turned upside down, all the water runs out so that it appears to be empty. When it is set back aright the water from the hollow sides refills the jug. Then the jug can pour more water. The jug can·refill itself several times. Magic jugs may be purchased at most novelty shops for about a dollar.*

I have here a jug of water. I want to use it to show you how God's grace works with us. Sometimes we have a hard time understanding words like that, so watch closely.

There are times when we do something we know we should not do. We may feel bad about it afterward, but we know that there is nothing we can do to *force* God's forgiveness. The Bible also tells us that there is no way we can *earn* God's forgiveness. All we can do is ask him. So we ask God to forgive us, and he pours out his love on us.

(Turn the jug completely upside down and pour

all the water into a glass. Shake the jug a little to let them see that there is no more water.)

That is how God forgives us.

(Pause for a few seconds to let the children reflect on God's willingness to forgive them.)

You all know what happens after awhile though. We accept God's forgiveness, but it is not long before we do something again and we need to be forgiven once more. But what can we do? We have already poured out all the water. That is when we really begin to see what God's grace is. Just when we think all of God's love is gone or used up, look what happens.

(Turn the jug upside down and pour out the water.)

There always seems to be a little more.

(Shake the jug again to demonstrate that it is "empty." This usually amazes the children.)

As we go through our lives we try to do what God asks; yet we continue to fall short of what we could be. Each time, however, God's grace always seems to have just a little more love ready for us whenever we are open to it.

(Pour out a little more water. The message can be continued as long as the jug can refill itself from the hollow sides.)

The thing to remember is this: God loves us! He tries to show us the best way to live because he knows that our lives will be happier if we live his way. When we fall short or disobey, God is always there, ready to help, ready to forgive. The love that he gives us, even when we think it should have run out, is called grace.

(Pour out more water from the "empty" jug.)

Always remember: God's love never stops!

The Firm Foundation

Text: *Matthew 7:24-27.*

Object: *A deck of cards and some clay.*

I have a deck of cards this morning. Out of these cards we are going to build something. I will take the cards, like this, and carefully set up the sides of a house.

(Begin putting them together.)

You can see how they all balance together. Now, very carefully, we put the roof on by laying the cards across the top. Now, it is finished. What do you think of our house? It has four walls and a nice roof. There is only one problem. Do you know what it is? Watch!

(Blow on the house.)

That is the problem. It will not stand up. No matter how many times we rebuild it, it will fall down every time the wind blows or something bumps it. Do you know why? I will tell you. The house does not have a foundation. The cards lean against one another, but they are not set into anything solid that will hold them when something tries to move them.

Watch what happens now. If I take four strips of this clay and place them in a square on the table, then press one side of a card in each of the strips, they now have a solid base. Now blow on the house. You see? They will not fall because they are set in the clay. They have what Jesus called a firm foundation. Without it, the cards will not stand. With it, they will not fall.

One day Jesus reminded a group of people that we build our lives just the way we build houses. We put them together and form a kind of emotional and spiritual home to live in. Like any other house, our emotional and spiritual house needs a foundation. It would be foolish to build one without a good foundation to hold us together when the problems come. As Christians, we know that the only real foundation for life is in doing what Jesus told us to do. If we live by his model and guide then we will have a firm foundation. If we build on anything else we will be like a house of cards. We look good for awhile, but when the wind blows we fall.

Let's remember, every time we see something solid, that we have the strongest thing in the world to build our lives on, and that is the God that Jesus showed us!

Once Too Often!

Text: *Galatians 6:2.*

Object: *A plastic camel. One may be found in the game called Breaking the Camel's Back. Or a camel can be made out of Tinker Toys, and the front and back halves connected with a rubber band that will stretch and cause the camel to fall under a heavy load.*

Everyone knows what this is; it is a plastic camel. As you can see, the camel has a little basket on each side, and the baskets are held together by a strap across his back. In that way he can carry a load. I also have here a pile of stick matches. That is the load I want the camel to carry. What I will do is put a few matches in each basket. (Do so.) See, the camel is still standing. He can carry that load without any problem.

Now I will put a few more matches in on each side. He is still doing fine. Maybe we can put in just one more, and just one more.

(Continue to add matches to each side until the rubber band holding the camel together begins to stretch and the camel's back begins to sag. Be sure to build up the suspense of how much the camel can hold. Finally, as you put the "last straw" in the basket, the rubber band will stretch and the two halves, front and back, will bend in the center and the camel's back will be broken.)

Oh! Now we've done it! Everything was fine until we added just that one more match. Now the camel is gone, and he cannot carry anything. Now we have lost it all just because we tried to add one more match. I think we should have stopped awhile back.

Do you know what we can learn from the camel? Right! We do the same thing with ourselves. We say, "I know I ought to stop, but just one more time cannot hurt." Then we do it once more, and once more, and we keep going until we do it once too often, and—BOOM!—we lose everything.

We all know what is the smart thing to do. When we are doing something that we know is not right, the thing to do is to stop before we add that one last straw.

This week, let's remember the camel and think about some of the things we do that we should not. Maybe we ought to stop before we end up like the camel.

It's as Big
as You Make It

Text: *Psalm 118:24.*

Object: *Two large sheets of white paper.*

Can you all see what I have here? What do you see?

(Let several children answer.)

That is right. It is a large sheet of white paper. Now I will take this ink pen and do this.

(Draw a small black dot in the center of the paper.)

Now tell me what you see. Bill sees a dot. So does John. Is that what the rest of you see? That is interesting. When you all look now, all you see is the dot. What about all the rest of the paper? Do you still see it? Then why didn't you mention it?

Have you ever thought that sometimes our entire lives are just like that? We start out a brand new day, just like this clean sheet of white paper.

(Hold up another clean sheet.)

It is clean and ready for anything. No one has ever lived it before. It is the beginning of a new life if we will let it be. Then one little thing will happen that we do not like. We may bump our toe, or someone may say something that we do not like. Someone may hurt our feelings. It could be any number of little things, and you know what happens.

(Draw a dot on the clean sheet.)

That is when we begin to do with our lives what we just did with the paper. We spend the rest of the day seeing only that little dot. We talk about it, we complain about it, and we let it become the center of our entire day. Then we say it was a "bad day." Doesn't that sound silly? I think we can all see how much better it would be if we would try to see not only the dot, but the rest of the paper as well.

God gives us a new day over and over again. We need to remember to use all of it, and not just concentrate on the little problems!

The Bible says, "This is the day that the Lord has made; let us rejoice and be glad." Each day is a whole new chance to see God's wonders. This week we surely will not be silly enough to let one little problem spoil an entire beautiful day.

Making Strong Walls

Text: *John 13:34-35.*

Object: *The wall of the church and some loose bricks.*

This morning I would like all of you to come over by the wall with me. As you can see, the wall is made of bricks. You may also have noticed that I have some loose bricks here on the floor. Watch carefully; I am going to build a wall right here out of these loose bricks. As you can see, all that is involved is setting one brick on top of another, like this. Now we have a little wall three bricks long and four bricks high. Does that look like a good solid wall to you? No? You think it would fall over if you pushed it? Why? Of course. There is no cement to hold the individual bricks together. That is what makes them strong, isn't it?

If you look back at the church wall you will notice that there is a cement bond between each brick. It is that bond that holds the bricks close to one another. You may also notice something else. Can you see how the bricks overlap one another? We can say, then, that the real difference between this strong wall and my pile of loose bricks is that the bricks in the church wall overlap one another, and they are plastered together firmly by cement.

Did you know that the same thing is true of people and the church? We can find a lot of people together in the same place, but that does not mean they are really close to one another or that they will help one another. What they have to have for that is a bond to draw them to one another. Christians know that bond is love. We know that God loves us and that we should share that love with one another. That is the cement that holds us together.

We are also involved with one another. That means that we help one another, and in so doing we are all made stronger.

There are many problems that can come up among people in a church, and different ideas about ways of doing things. If we were just a pile of loose bricks, we might fall apart. That cannot happen when we are held together by love, however. Love is the strongest bond in the world. It makes us strong, and we join together in working for common goals.

Whenever we are in a class or with our friends and we are trying to settle problems, let's remember one thing for sure: no problem can be more important than the bond of love among us.

It Took Some Thought

Text: *Psalm 19:1.*

Object: *A pocket watch.*

This is what some people call a family heirloom. That is something that has been passed down in the family for a long time. It is a pocket watch. It belonged to my grandfather, my father, and now to me. I want to show you something interesting about this watch.

(Open the back of the watch and let the children each take a turn at looking at the many small wheels and springs.)

That really looks complicated, doesn't it?

(You may want to spend some time at this point explaining the manner in which a watch works.)

Do you know how this was made? Well, I am going to tell you. One day a man was working with a great pile of little pieces of metal, wheels and springs and such, and he dropped some of them off the edge of the table and onto the floor. They all landed with a great thud! When he bent down to pick them up, he discovered that the pieces had fallen in such a way that they created this watch on the way down. All these wheels just happened to fall into the right place and started

49

keeping time all by themselves, by accident. What do you think of that?

What? You do not believe me? Why not? You think that something so complicated and yet so smooth-running must have taken a lot of thought and planning. Of course it did! The man who made this watch put a great deal of thought and effort into it.

Now do you want to know something that will really seem silly? There are some people who think our world and all the planets and stars were created by accident, and they just happen to run perfectly because that is the way the accident went.

Can you imagine, believing that a simple thing like a watch had to be planned, that something as complicated and as perfect as our universe happened by chance? Not very likely, is it?

From now on, whenever you see a watch or a piece of machinery, spend some time thinking about God and all the marvelous creations of his. From the small insects, so tiny we need a microscope to see them, to the planets and star systems that are so huge we cannot see their limits even with the most powerful telescopes, God made it all, and everything works perfectly. What a tremendous creation it is!

There is one thing that is especially interesting about all this, however. You can see all the wheels and springs in the watch. Do you know what would happen if one of the parts was removed? It would not run right, would it?

Just like the parts of the watch, every part of God's creation is important. Even with all of the millions of parts in his creation, each of us is important. God created everything and everyone, and we all have a part to play. That makes us a part of God's work, and means we should always do our best to fulfill his call.

He Can See It All

Text: *Psalm 23.*

Object: *A fairly large throw rug with a design or picture woven into it.*

As you can see, I have a rug all folded up in my lap. Before I unfold it I would like one of you boys to step forward and stand very still with your eyes closed. I am going to hold the rug close to your nose; then I want you to open your eyes.

Now, with the rug right next to your nose, tell us what you see. That's right. You see some red, some blue, and a little yellow. Do you see anything else? No. That is because you are so close. When you are right up next to it, all you can see are a few colors, but you cannot see the entire picture.

If I move the rug away from you, look how much more of it you can see. Now you can tell us what the entire picture is. That seems simple, doesn't it?

Do you know what we can learn from this? There are many times when we cannot understand why certain things happen the way they do. There are some things that God tells us in the Bible that we might think are useless or do not make much sense. It is like looking at the rug close up. We can see little patches of green or red, but they do not make any sense to us. We wonder why they are there. Then, as we get farther away from the rug, we begin to see that all the colors we did not understand actually fit into a pattern or picture. When we have the whole picture, the parts make sense to us.

That was the kind of trust David had when he thought about God. He knew that sometimes he would be in places that seemed like beautiful green pastures, calm and peaceful. At other times he would be somewhere that was like a valley of death. There would be things that he did not understand and things that would bother him greatly. But in those times he was not afraid. He did his best to learn and understand, and, above all, he knew that God was there to help and guide him like a shepherd. David knew that God could see all of what was happening, and he trusted God to do what was best for him.

When we begin to feel that God has forgotten us, or when we think his guidance is wrong, we ought to remember the rug, and the experience of David. We are living one day at a time, and we can only see a little piece of what is happening. God, on the other hand, can see everything that is going on. He knows the whole pattern and therefore knows what is best. Sometimes, as time passes, we can see that God knew best, even though at the time we were not so sure.

So the next time you wonder why God tells you to act certain ways or do certain things that you may not understand, remember the rug. We can only see a small part of it. God sees the whole picture and knows what is best.

Everyone Has a Place

Text: *I Corinthians 12:14-27.*

Object: *Several ball-point pens. The major object is a pointer pen. This is a pointer that telescopes down into what appears to be a ball-point pen. It is carried in the pocket and is brought out and pulled to its full length when ready to use. It can be purchased at most stationery stores.*

This morning I have a handful of ball-point pens. As you can see, they are all different kinds and colors. If we take this first one and try to write with it (attempt to write on the paper), nothing happens. Oh! I have to push this little button on the top first. When I push it down the point comes out. Now the pen is useful, isn't it?

If I take the second pen, push the button on top, and . . . nothing happens. Why not? There is no point. Oh. To get the point out of this one I have to twist the top of the pen. That is different, but it still works. I guess we can keep it too.

Here is a third one, and it is different from the other two. I have seen it before. To get the point out of this one we have to slide this button on the side. It does work, however.

Now let's take a look at this silver one. If I push the button on the top . . . nothing happens. Let's try twisting it. No, nothing happened then, either. Maybe the clip part slides. No, that did not do it, either. Does anyone have any ideas?

(Let several of the children make suggestions, and try them to see if they will work.)

No. Nothing seems to work. What do you think we ought to do? Maybe we ought to just throw this one away. It will not write. I guess there is no use for it.

(Allow the children time to nod their agreement.)

On the other hand, if someone made it there must be some use for it. You know, just because something does not fit the kind of pattern we expect it to does not mean that it is useless. Let's see if there is something the pen can do.

(Spend some time examining the pen very closely.)

Look at this! I have discovered something. If I pull on the end of the pen it stretches, farther and farther. How about that! It may not work as a pen, but it certainly has a use. It is a pointer. That has lots of uses. Just think. A minute ago we were going to throw it away. We almost made a terrible mistake. Just because it did not act the way we thought it should we were going to say it was no good.

Now we know it may be the best of all, when we let it fill its own special purpose.

If you think about it, you may realize that we often do the same thing with people. We expect them all to act the same way and do the same things. We expect them to dress alike, go the same places, even like the same food. Then we meet someone who is different. We try to get him to do things that everyone else does, and in the same way, but it does not seem to work. That is when we decide to throw him away. Of course we cannot throw people away, but we can ignore them. We refuse to play with them or just pretend they are not there.

What we should learn from the pointer pen is that everyone has something to offer and share. Everyone is special in his own way. What we need to do is get to know him and find what he can do, then help him to do it to the best of his ability. That is what Jesus did, and that is what we are called to do in his name.

The next time you see someone who is different, remember the pointer. We do not condemn people for being different. We enjoy the new things they can show us.

Slowing Down
Doesn't Help

Text: *Ezekiel 18:30.*

Object: *A toy car and a fairly long board.*

I have here a board. I want you to pretend with me that it is a road. At the end of this road, where the board stops, we will pretend there is a great cliff. As you can see, it is a long drop to the floor.

I also have a little car. We can drive the car along the road very slowly. It runs very smoothly and the driver inside is having a nice ride. There is a problem, though, isn't there? What is going to happen if the car keeps going? That's right. It is going to fall off the edge and be broken, and the driver will be hurt or killed.

We do not want that to happen, so we call to the driver and warn him about the cliff. We say, "Watch out! If you keep going that way you will fall off the cliff and be hurt." We can also pretend that the driver heard us. Do you know what he replied? He said we should not worry, he would just slow down a little bit. What do you think of that? That's silly, isn't it? He is still going in the wrong direction. He is going slower, but he is still headed in the direction of the cliff. The only way he can keep from going off the edge is to stop, turn around, and go the other way. That is the smart thing to do.

Have you ever thought that God sees us the same way? That is what Ezekiel was saying in the verse we read. Many times God sees us doing things we should not do, or heading in directions that will lead us into trouble, and we hear his voice inside us saying, "You should not do that. If you keep going in that way you will be hurt."

God says that to us, and so many times we are just like our man in the car. We say we really do not need to stop, we will just slow down a little, or we will not do it quite so often. But you can see that will not work. We are going slower, but, like the man in the car, we are still headed in the wrong direction: toward the cliff. The only thing we can do to be really safe is stop, turn around, and go the other way. That is what the Bible means by "repent": to stop doing what is wrong and to do what God wants us to do.

He tells us what to do as we talk to him in prayer, as we read his Word in the Bible, and also in the little voice we hear so often inside us. So the next time you hear his voice saying, "Do not

59

go that way," remember the man in the car. It does not do any good to say we are just going to slow down. We have to stop and go the other way. God sends us in directions that are safe, because he loves us.

Eating Away

Text: *Matthew 12:43-45.*

Object: *Two pieces of wood, one with the inside eaten away by termites.*

We are thinking about putting up some shelves in the church, and I have some of the wood here. They will be holding some heavy material, so we had to get good strong wood. These two pieces both look strong and solid. Feel this one. You can feel how hard and solid it is. It ought to hold a great deal of weight.

(Give them the solid one to hold and examine.)

This other piece looks just as good, doesn't it? You can run your hand over the surface and see how it feels. It may even be a little prettier than the other piece. So we can say, from all appearances, we have two good pieces of wood.

Now let me show you something.

(Break the termite-eaten board in half.)

What do you think of that? We can see now that while both boards looked good on the outside, one of them was eaten up by termites on the inside. One was strong, while the other was just a shell.

We can learn something very important from these boards. What is true for boards is also true for people. God gives us a good firm way to live

61

nside his guidelines. Then along comes a
n. It may seem like just a little one, like
e termite. It does not look very dangerous,
o not worry about it. Then it gets inside us
and begins to eat, and it even begins to invite some
of its friends. They all get busy, and they eat away
a little here and a little there. We say they are just
little sins, or little habits, that are not really important, but after awhile we are just like the board.
We look good on the outside, but our inner strength
is gone. When something big happens and we try
to draw on the strength inside us we find ourselves
broken, like the board.

That was the point that Jesus was trying to il-
lustrate when he told the story about the man who
thought he had his life all in order. It was all swept
and clean, but then he found that while he was
not paying attention the "termites" came in and
took over.

How do we keep this from happening? We have
to do the same thing with little sins and habits
that we do with termites. As soon as we see one
trying to move in we need to drive it out, otherwise it will take us over. If we stop these little sins
one at a time as they come in, they are no problem
and we remain the way God wants us, not only
good on the outside, but strong and whole on the
inside as well.

Fists

Text: *Proverbs 3:30.*

Object: *A bag of candy and a volunteer.*

I need a volunteer. Will you help please?
(Pick one of the boys.)

Now all I want you to do is to make a fist with each hand. That is the way. Now, no matter what happens I want you to keep your fists clenched as tight as you can, all right? Good.

While he is doing that, I would like the rest of the children to see that I have something to give our volunteer for being nice enough to help me. I have a bag of candy.

(Eat a piece and give some to a few of the other children, but do not give any to the volunteer.)

That is good candy, isn't it?

Now I would like our volunteer to have some. You may take some out of the bag, but remember to keep your fists as tight as you can make them.

(Let him try to take some out. He will, of course, not be able to do so.)

What is the problem? I keep trying to give you some of the candy. All the rest of the children can see that I am offering it to you. Why don't you take some? Oh. You cannot get any out because your fists are clenched. Well, open your hand and see what happens. Now you can get some without any trouble. That's a little better, isn't it?

You know, we can learn something important from all this. There are many times in life, in each day, when people try to give us things. They may be trying to give us something we can see, like this candy, or it may be something we cannot see, like their friendship or their help. They may want to give us a smile or just be nice. But if we are angry, or have our emotional fists clenched, we cannot receive what they are trying to give us, just as John could not get the candy even though I was offering it to him.

This week, let's spend some time each day asking ourselves how we meet other people. Do we open ourselves up and act friendly, or do we close up like a fist and stay apart? We all know we are happier with our hands open so we can both give and receive.

The Missing Pieces

Text: *Hebrews 10:23-25.*

Object: *A child's puzzle of about twenty pieces.*

I want you all to gather around this little table for a few minutes and help me work this puzzle. You all know how puzzles work. We have a lot of little pieces, all of which are different. If we hold up just one piece it does not look like much, does it? What happens, though, if we begin joining some of the pieces together? Now we begin to get a picture.

(Put the pieces you have together. Have five or six of the pieces in your pocket.)

There! How do you like the picture? It looks all right, but something is wrong. The picture is not complete, is it? Several of the pieces are missing. That ruins the whole picture. It could be very nice, but with some of the pieces gone, all we see are the holes.

(Let the children comment on the problem the holes cause.)

Now what happens if I put in the missing pieces?

(Put each one in, commenting on how much

better the picture looks with the addition of each missing piece.)

Now the puzzle is complete. It is everything it should be. When all the pieces are in place it makes a very pretty picture, doesn't it?

There is still one more thing I want you to do, however. I want you all to stand up, turn around, and look out over the congregation. It looks a little like our puzzle with the pieces missing, doesn't it? There are a lot of holes where people ought to be.

You can see from this that each of us has a very important part to play in making the church what it should be. When we do not come, or when we fail to do our part, we are just like a missing piece of a puzzle. Not only is there a hole, but also a particular and important part of the picture is missing. We should always remember that each of us is important; we are never missing without being missed.

Being God's Helper

Text: *Acts 20:35.*

Object: *A dime and appropriate pictures.*

Can you all see this dime? Here, I want some of you to feel it. Can you bend it? See if you can make it into a ball. Maybe you can press it down into the size of a seed, or a piece of rice. You think that is silly? It really is not. You may not know it, but a dime can change its shape. Let me show you. Did you know that a dime could look like this?

(Show a picture of a bowl of rice.)

It can. When we use it through our missionaries we can turn it into food or medicine or even clothes. We can also turn a dime into a toy or a candy bar. The question for Christians is, How are we going to use it?

That is what Christians call stewardship. Money itself is not what is important. We cannot eat it or wear it. It is important because of what we can turn it into. So how we treat our dimes is very important.

Do we go off and buy a candy bar, or do we remember that our dime can be turned into food for someone who may otherwise go hungry? Do we buy another little toy that we really do not need, or do we turn the money into medicine for a child who would otherwise have to go without help?

The thing we need to ask ourselves when we have money is, What can this become? We are Jesus' money changers. We turn coins into help for the people God loves. Jesus tells us that we have a happier feeling when we give things than when we receive. We may not understand that at first, but when we begin to see the wonderful things our dimes can become we know what it means to be God's helper. That is the greatest thing in the world.

This week, each time we start to spend some money, let's ask ourselves what it could become and whom it could help if we would let it.

Stretching the Point

Text: *Romans 6:1-2.*

Object: *A rubber band.*

This morning I am going to need a volunteer. I would like you to hold one end of this rubber band. I will hold the other end. Now, if I stretch this rubber band it will snap and hurt you, right? Of course.

(At this point stretch the rubber band slightly.)

Look, I stretched it and nothing happened. Was I wrong? Maybe it will not snap after all. Let's stretch it a little more and see.

(Stretch it again slightly. Repeat this action several times. Each time you stretch the rubber band, make a point of the fact that it did not break. Finally on the last tug, let it go.)

Oh! I bet that stung your finger. I guess I was right. If you stretch the rubber band far enough it will snap.

You know, we might be able to learn something from that rubber band. God tells us if we do certain things, we will be hurt. If we steal, we will be hurt because others will not trust us. If we cheat, others will not play with us. By breaking God's Word we hurt ourselves as well as others.

Sometimes we break God's law once, and nothing seems to happen, like the first time we stretched the rubber band. Then we think God must be wrong, so we do it once more, like the second time we stretched the rubber band. We keep saying, I will just do it one more time. Then all of a sudden —SNAP! Then we are hurt, and possibly some other people as well. You know what we usually do then? We try to blame everyone else for what happened to us. We thought just because we did not get hurt the first time, we could go on forever.

The lesson the rubber band can teach us is that just because we seem to get away with something once, that does not make it right. It is only a matter of time before we will have to pay for it. The wise thing to do is to obey God in the first place and listen to what he says.

The Source of Power

Text: *Acts 1:8.*

Object: *A desk lamp.*

Some of you may have seen this lamp in the office. It is a new desk lamp. It is just the kind of lamp I have always wanted. As you can see, it has everything it needs. It has a beautiful design. The shade is perfect. It has all the switches and cords it needs, and I have a brand new bulb that is just the right size. I believe we can say it is perfect! You can see how well it works.

(Attempt to turn it on.)

What is wrong? Nothing happened. The bulb is there, the cord is all right. All the switches are working. What can the problem be?

(Let the children look it over and provide various suggestions.)

Ah! You have spotted it. The cord is not plugged in. If I put the plug into this wall socket, let's see what happens. Now it works! The lamp was all right, it just didn't have a source of power.

Did you know that people are just like this lamp in that regard? Most of us have all the abilities we need to do a fine job for our family or church. We have healthy minds and bodies, good intentions, and we try hard; yet something is missing. Do you know what it is? We are not plugged into God's power line.

Christians know that the power of God comes through the Holy Spirit. We learned that at Pentecost. Jesus knew that his disciples had the will to work for him and that they had all the tools they needed. Yet he told them that they were still lacking one thing: a direct power supply. Like the lamp, the Disciples, and you and I, have to be plugged into God's Holy Spirit before we have the power to do what he wants done.

This power of the Spirit is a gift from God, and we should ask him each day to guide us as we try to live exactly as the Bible tells us. When we begin each day with prayer, and spend time each day reading God's Word, then we begin to open ourselves to God's Spirit. Then we begin to receive the power to do the task he set for us.

Let's spend some time each day asking God to guide us and show us how to live.

God's Road Map

Text: *Joshua 1:8-9.*

Object: *A road map of the United States.*

I do not know if any of you have ever tried to follow a map, but I know all of you have seen maps. This is a map of the United States. When we look at the map, we can see that we are right here at this dot. Let's say we wanted to plan a trip to Chicago—that is the dot way over there. We can see that there are several lines going between us and Chicago. Each one of them represents a road. To get to Chicago we would have to follow some of these lines. Now we have everything that we need. We know where we are: here. We also know where we want to go: over to here. The most important thing is that we also know how to get there: by following the roads.

Now, having all these directions, let's plan our trip. We can begin here, where we live, and start out going this way.

(Run your finger on a road going the opposite direction from Chicago. One of the children will notice it and call it to your attention.)

What? What do you mean, that's wrong? I am following a road. Oh, I see. I am following a road, but not the *right* road. It is taking me the wrong

75

way. If we really wanted to go to Chicago it would be foolish if we went in the opposite direction. We would never get where we wanted to go, would we?

If it would be foolish on a short trip, think how much more foolish it would be to do that with our lives; but sometimes we do.

We know what we are like now. When we see Jesus, we know how we would like to be. To become like Jesus, we need a guide, a sort of a map. The Bible is the road map that tells us how to get where we want to be. So if the path is set out for us, we need to follow it. If we do something different from what it says, then we are going in the opposite direction. That means that no matter how hard we work, or how fast we go, it really does not help. We are going in the wrong direction. Just like the map—until we begin to follow the right lines, we will never get where we want to go. That is why Jesus and the early church left us the Bible. It is our road map. As long as we follow it, we are going in the right direction and we will get where we want to be: like Jesus. When we begin to go in other ways, we are still moving, but we are not headed toward our goal.

This week, let's spend some time each day looking at the map God gave us. It is our guide, and if we let it, it will show us the way to God.

How Do We Say Thank You?

Text: *Acts 20:35.*

Object: *Candy.*

You all know that today is Thanksgiving Sunday. You also know that Thanksgiving is a day when we say "thank you" for all the good things that God and others have given us.

Well, today I want to say "thank you" to all of you. I enjoy talking with you very much. To show you how thankful I am, I have brought some candy in this bag. Do you know what I am going to do? Well, to show you how much I appreciate your coming down, I am going to sit here and eat this candy.

(Begin eating, but make no effort to share any with the children. Simply smile and eat for a few minutes.)

Why do you look so confused? I told you I was thanking you. Do you not like the way I am doing it? Why not? You think I ought to give you some of the candy? Why? Oh, because you are the ones who are being thanked. Well, that does seem reasonable. But now think for just a moment. Isn't this exactly what most of us do on Thanksgiving day? We say we are going to be thankful to God, but all we really do sit down and eat everything we can find.

Do you think maybe God might feel the same way you did? Maybe he is saying, "If you really want to say thank you, learn to share some of the things you have; don't just stuff yourself!"

God gives freely to us, and he calls us to share those gifts with others. This week let's really be thankful, and when we think of someone who has done something nice for us, take some time to let him know you appreciate it. To be *truly thankful* we must *truly thank* someone. We can begin with God, and thank him by doing his will toward others.

Sending a Savior

Text: *John 3:16.*

Object: *A glass ant farm.*

Can you all see what I have in this glass box? Ants.
I have a whole colony of ants. We can all see that
they are busy building their homes and doing the
things ants do. But there is a problem that the ants
do not know about. They are going to have to leave
their glass home and move into this other box because there is a germ in the soil of their house that
will kill them if they stay there.

What I would like one of you to do is to explain
that to the ants. It is the only thing that will save
them. Who would like to try? Who can think of a
way to communicate with them?

(Let several of the children try to figure out some
way to lead the ants to safety.)

Nothing seems to work. There is nothing we can
do to reach the ants. I guess they are all going to
die, and there is nothing we can do about it. But
let me ask just one more question. What if you
could become ants like them? Then you could talk
to them in their own way. You could be one of
them and lead them to a better place. In fact, we
know from what we have just tried that the *only*

way you could save them would be to become ants like them.

Did you know that that is exactly what God did for us? He knew that we could not really live a full and eternal life without his guidance and the power he gives us. When he tried to show us the way through prophets and his commandments, people just could not seem to understand.

Finally God decided that the only way really to reach people was to become one of us, the way we wanted to become one of the ants. That is how much he loves us.

That is what happened on the first Christmas. Every year we remember again that God loves us so much that he sent his only Son, Jesus, to show us the way to Eternal Life.